D1535979

Our American Family™

I Am Mexican American

Isobel Seymour

The Rosen Publishing Group's
PowerKids Press™
New York

Published in 1997 by The Rosen Publishing Group, Inc.
29 East 21st Street, New York, NY 10010

First Edition

Book Design: Erin McKenna

Photo Credits: Cover © Noble Stock/International Stock Photo; pp. 4, 19 © Rob Gage/FPG International Corp.; p. 7 © Telegraph Colour Library/FPG International Corp.; p. 8 © Suzanne Murphy/FPG International Corp.; p. 11 © Haroldo de Faria Castro/FPG International Corp.; p. 12 © Bruce Stoddard /FPG International Corp.; p. 15 © Victor Scocozza/FPG International Corp.; p. 16 © Lee Langum/FPG International Corp.; p. 20 © Vladimir Pcholkin/FPG International Corp.

Seymour, Isobel.
    I am Mexican American / by Isobel Seymour.
        p.   cm. — (Our American Family)
    Includes index.
    Summary: A Mexican-American child talks about aspects of his Mexican heritage, including language, foods, and customs.
    ISBN 0-8239-5004-2
    1. Mexican Americans—Juvenile literature. [1. Mexican Americans.]
    I. Title. II. Series.
E184.M5S77 1997
973'.046872—dc21   96-54231
    JS   CIP
                                                          AC

Manufactured in the United States of America

Contents

Luis

Hola (OH-la)! My name is Luis, and my family is Mexican American. My grandparents came to America from a small village in Mexico. I live with my parents and three sisters in Los Angeles, California. Because we were all born in the United States, we are American **citizens** (SIH-tih-zenz). But my parents think it's very important for us to learn about the history and **culture** (KUL-cher) of both Mexico and America.

◀ Have you ever asked your family where you and your relatives came from?

Mexico

Mexico is a country that borders the United States. The northern part of Mexico is connected to part of the southern U.S. Along with Canada, Mexico and the United States make up the **continent** (KON-tin-ent) of North America.

Mexico is divided into 31 states. Mexico City is the capital of the country. The head of the Mexican government is the president. The biggest cities are very crowded, but most Mexicans still live in small towns.

Mexico is full of historic buildings, such as the ▶
Mexico City Museum of Art in Mexico City.

Coming to America

Life was hard for my grandparents in Mexico. There were very few jobs, and there wasn't enough to eat. My grandparents often heard that America had plenty of jobs and food, so they came here. For a long time, things were just as hard for them in the United States. My grandparents picked fruit and vegetables for farmers. They worked long hours in the hot sun. They hardly ever saw their families. But they stayed in the U.S. because they knew life would be better for their children and grandchildren.

◀ Many Mexicans worked long hours on farms in the United States.

9

Spanish

The official language of Mexico is Spanish. People who come from Spanish-speaking countries are called **Hispanic** (his-PAN-ik). My sisters and I go to a **bilingual** (by-LING-wul) school. That means we speak two languages there—Spanish and English. Our morning classes are held in Spanish, and our afternoon classes are in English. Many English words come from Spanish. Two of my favorite ones are chocolate and vanilla!

◀ Mexican schoolchildren learn many of the same subjects in school as American children do.

13

Food

My parents own a Mexican restaurant. They serve some of the same foods that we eat at home. Many Mexican dishes are made with **tortillas** (tor-TEE-yuhz). Tortillas are flat breads that are often folded and stuffed with meat or vegetables. Tacos, burritos, and **enchiladas** (en-chil-AH-dahz) are all made with tortillas. Mexican foods are also often made with rice, beans, and very spicy chili peppers.

Mexican food is full of different spices and flavors. You ▶ can see tacos, nachos, and fajitas in this picture.

Mexican Art

My Aunt Rosa is an artist. I call her *Tia* (TEE-ya), which means "aunt" in Spanish. She makes a lot of traditional Mexican folk art. She especially likes to make pottery. Sometimes she lets me help her. We take wet clay and shape it into vases or plates. Then we put the dried clay pieces in a kiln, or pottery oven, to bake them. Once they've been baked, or fired, we paint Mexican designs on them.

◀ Mexican artists often use bright colors and patterns in their work.

Piñatas

My aunt also makes **piñatas** (peen-YA-tas) for all of our **fiestas** (fee-ES-tuhz). Any Mexican celebration is called a fiesta. Some piñatas are made of colored paper, but Tia Rosa always makes clay piñatas shaped like animals. She leaves a hole in the bottom of it so my parents can fill it with candy and little toys. We hang the piñata from the ceiling and cover our eyes with a blindfold. Then everyone takes turns trying to hit it with a stick. When it breaks, all the stuffing falls out and everybody runs to get some!

Piñatas are often a part of special celebrations, such as birthday parties. ▶

Christmas

Nearly all Mexicans are Catholic, including my family. Christmas is a very important holiday for us. In fact, we start celebrating it on December 16. Every night, from that day until Christmas Eve, my family and our friends have parties where we act out the Christmas story. On Christmas Day, we all go to church together. We don't give each other presents until January 6, which is called Dia de los Reyes, or Day of the Kings.

◀ Going to church is an important part of Christmas Day for many Catholic people. Some go to tiny chapels and others go to large cathedrals.

I Am Mexican American

My parents have taught my sisters and me to be proud of our Mexican and American **heritages** (HEHR-ih-tij-ez). In school and at home, we speak both Spanish and English. We also learn about the histories of both Mexico and the United States. We're lucky we can combine these two cultures. One day I hope to visit the village in Mexico where my grandparents came from. I'm proud to be Mexican American.

Glossary

ancestor (AN-ses-ter) A family member who lived before you.

bilingual (by-LING-wul) Able to speak two languages.

citizen (SIH-tih-zen) Someone who is a member of a country.

continent (KON-tin-ent) A very large body of land.

culture (KUL-cher) The beliefs, customs, and religions of a group of people.

enchilada (en-chil-AH-dah) A Mexican dish in which beans or meat and cheese are wrapped in a tortilla.

fiesta (fee-ES-tuh) A Mexican celebration.

heritage (HEHR-ih-tij) The cultural traditions that are handed down from parent to child.

Hispanic (his-PAN-ik) From a Spanish-speaking country.

hola (OH-la) The Spanish word for "hello."

mestizo (mes-TEE-zoh) A mix of Spanish and Native American backgrounds.

piñata (peen-YA-ta) A clay or paper object filled with candy and toys.

tia (TEE-ya) The Spanish word for "aunt."

tortilla (tor-TEE-yuh) A flat bread made from corn or flour.

tradition (truh-DISH-un) The customs, beliefs, and religions that are passed down from parent to child.

Index

24